QuoteOctopus.com

The best quotes

Publisher Contact

257 Swanston Street, Melbourne, VIC, AUSTRALIA

Email: hello@quoteoctopus.com

Social media: facebook.com/quoteoctopus

Acknowledgements

The team at Quote Octopus would like to thank our friends, family, suppliers and customers for making our vision of creating the highest-quality books a reality. Thanks for purchasing and enjoy the quotes!

This page is intentionally left blank

This page is intentionally left blank

'Never Have Your Dog Stuffed' is really advice to myself, a reminder to myself not to avoid change or uncertainty, but to go with it, to surf into change.

Alan Alda

A really great actor, in a lucky performance, can transform himself or herself. I've seen actors do that. But often it's a mechanical transformation, which isn't as interesting, and you've got to be careful how you go about something like that, I think.

Alan Alda

Achingly funny as it was, Larry Gelbart's writing gave off sparks that turned a hard light on the way we are.

Alan Alda

After a while I started to think of that as an image of something that went a lot deeper than the dead dog, which is you can't bring back anything to life.

Alan Alda

All I've ever tried to do is play real people.

Alan Alda

Almost everybody that's well-known gets tagged with a nickname.

Alan Alda

And I think belief is one of those things that comes to people in their own way. And just because I believe in something doesn't mean I think that you should.

Alan Alda

Any play is hard to write, and plays are getting harder and harder to get on the stage.

Alan Alda

Anyone I know who's almost died has come out of it, at least for a while, looking at things differently.

Alan Alda

As an artist, as an actor, as a writer, you have to use what's personal to you. You have to be personal about your work; otherwise, it doesn't ring true.

Alan Alda

Awards can give you a tremendous amount of encouragement to keep getting better, no matter how young or old you are.

Alan Alda

Awards shows mainly publicize the people giving the awards.

Alan Alda

Backstage life is terrific training for an actor, seeing shows from the wings.

Alan Alda

Be as smart as you can, but remember that it is always better to be wise than to be smart.

Alan Alda

Be brave enough to live life creatively. The creative place where no one else has ever been.

Alan Alda

Be fair with others, but then keep after them until they're fair with you.

Alan Alda

Begin challenging your assumptions. Your assumptions are the windows on the world. Scrub them off every once in awhile or the light won't come in.

Alan Alda

Begin challenging your own assumptions. Your assumptions are your windows on the world. Scrub them off every once in while, or the light won't come in.

Alan Alda

Blind dates are treacherous. You don't know who this person is. You wonder, 'Should I call my grandma during coffee to get out of this?'

Alan Alda

For me, I find that even though I've accomplished a few things in my life, looking back on accomplishments doesn't give me a sense of satisfaction.

Alan Alda

Here's my Golden Rule for a tarnished age: Be fair with others, but keep after them until they're fair with you.

Alan Alda

I always loved Sid Caesar and all the people on his program.

Alan Alda

I come armed with a really good ignorance. I don't strive toward ignorance. I come by it naturally.

Alan Alda

I don't miss directing at all, and I don't miss screenwriting either because somebody's always telling you to do something different.

Alan Alda

I don't really worry about the size of the part much any more. It's nice to have more time to work on the character, and to have big scenes to play. But if there's something playable there, and if it's interesting to do, then that's nice.

Alan Alda

I don't watch that much TV, so I can't compare one show to another. When I watch television, I watch people talking to one another usually or a science show where they show me microbes, you know. Microbes actually communicate quite a bit, and so there's a lot of talking going on.

Alan Alda

I feel like every time a door is opened by science, suddenly there are a hundred doors that need to get opened. That's what makes it an everlasting, interesting experience to go through.

Alan Alda

I find myself going to places where I really have no business, speaking to these people in a whole other field that I have no extensive knowledge of. But I do it very often because it scares me.

Alan Alda

I fix my grandchildren's computers.

Alan Alda

I found I wasn't asking good enough questions because I assumed I knew something. I would box them into a corner with a badly formed question, and they didn't know how to get out of it. Now, I let them take me through it step by step, and I listen.

Alan Alda

I had never really wanted to be famous. Everyone is supposed to want to be rich and famous, but as a boy I never knew what rich was, and the first view I had of famous made me leery.

Alan Alda

I hated high school. It was a prison.

Alan Alda

I have a strong preference for being alive.

Alan Alda

I know there's a creative side to artists to - pardon me - there's a creative side to scientists already, but there may be an artistic side, too, waiting to break free.

Alan Alda

I love oatmeal. To me, it's not boring. I agree that ordinary oatmeal is very boring, but not the steel-cut Irish kind - the kind that pops in your mouth when you bite into it in little glorious bursts like a sort of gummy champagne.

Alan Alda

I love technology.

Alan Alda

I love to watch how scientists' minds work.

Alan Alda

I made my first stage appearance when I was 6 months old.

Alan Alda

I must have interviewed 600 or 700 scientists all around the world.

Alan Alda

I never thought about my image. It interests me that there are people who do, that they seem to be methodical about it. Maybe things would have gone differently for me in some ways if I had.

Alan Alda

I read science, because to me, that's extremely exciting. It's like a great detective story, and it's happening right in front of us.

Alan Alda

I really don't like plays or movies that service propaganda.

Alan Alda

I sat next to a young woman on a plane once who bombarded me for five hours with how she had decided to be born again and so should I. I told her I was glad for her, but I hadn't used up being born the first time.

Alan Alda

I think I look better in a suit than a loincloth. So that may define some of the parts I play.

Alan Alda

I think it's important for scientists to speak in their own voices and not just be mediated by journalists or others speaking for them.

Alan Alda

I think most people are interested in our origins; once we understand, it might be easier to become the people we'd like to be. Or, better, become the people we think we already are.

Alan Alda

I think when you're acting, you usually don't have to know too much beyond how to pronounce the words you're saying.

Alan Alda

I used to be a Catholic. I left because I object to conversion by concussion. If you don't agree with what they teach, you get clobbered over the head until you do. All that does is change the shape of the head.

Alan Alda

I used to be an amateur inventor when I was a kid; I'm always inventing something.

Alan Alda

I used to not want to die in any way but in my sleep when I was a young man. I'd like to die awake now, if possible, with people around me who love me.

Alan Alda

I used to read science fiction a lot, and I still like science fiction when it is a model of how we really are and to see ourselves from another perspective.

Alan Alda

I was a child, and my mother was psychotic. She loved me, but I didn't really feel I had a mother. And when you live with somebody who is paranoid and thinks you're trying to kill them all the time, you tend to feel a little betrayed.

Alan Alda

I was always interested in figuring things out. I'd do experiments, like combining things I found around the house to see what would happen if I put them together.

Alan Alda

I was brought up as a Catholic, and I'm no longer a Catholic. I don't talk about my beliefs too much in public probably because I feel very strongly that it's something personal - more than personal, it's private.

Alan Alda

I would like to know that when I read the paper in the morning, it's telling me something that actually happened, and I think the vast majority of journalists want the same thing.

Alan Alda

I wouldn't live in California. All that sun makes you sterile.

Alan Alda

I'm an angry person, angrier than most people would imagine, I get flashes of anger. What works for me is working out when it's useful to use that anger.

Alan Alda

I'm condemned by some inner compulsion to think about the daily rituals of my life. I have a low grade fever for improving myself in many ways, including everyday tasks.

Alan Alda

I'm greedy for that satisfaction of doing something hard and knowing that, even though I was afraid I couldn't do it, that somehow I can deliver.

Alan Alda

I'm in the real world, some people try to steal from me, and I stop them, frequently, take them to court. I love a good lawsuit. It's fun.

Alan Alda

I'm most at home on the stage. I was carried onstage for the first time when I was six months old.

Alan Alda

I've been lucky enough to live through all the things that are supposed to give meaning to our lives, like parenting, grandparenting, art, celebrity. All these things you expect meaning to come from, and sometimes it comes when you're not expecting it.

Alan Alda

I've been nominated twice before as actor in a leading part. Now I'm nominated as actor in a supporting part. If I don't win, I'll just wait until I'm nominated for being in the theater during the show. Do they have one like that?

Alan Alda

I've had many uncanny experiences. I think it's hard to be alive and not have them. But I don't know if I can decide what that means or what they are.

Alan Alda

I've never tried to manipulate my image.

Alan Alda

I've sat looking down into a volcano that could blow at any moment; I've helped catch a shark and several rattlesnakes; I let a tarantula walk across my hand, and I ate rat soup.

Alan Alda

If I can't get the girl, at least give me more money.

Alan Alda

If scientists can't communicate with the public, with policy makers, with one another, the future is going to be held back. We're not going to have the future that we could have.

Alan Alda

If scientists could communicate more in their own voices - in a familiar tone, with a less specialized vocabulary - would a wide range of people understand them better? Would their work be better understood by the general public, policy-makers, funders, and, even in some cases, other scientists?

Alan Alda

If two scientists are giving their papers at a symposium, and one of them is just naturally better at talking to the public or talking to a group of people, that scientist is liable to get more attention - in fact, I'm told that they do get more attention - than the one who's a little more stiff about it. Well, that's not good for science.

Alan Alda

In 2003, I almost died of an intestinal blockage when I was on a mountain in Chile, filming a segment for 'Scientific American Frontiers.'

Alan Alda

In the midst of the sense of tragedy or loss, sometimes laughter is not only healing, it's a way of experiencing the person that you've lost again.

Alan Alda

It isn't necessary to be rich and famous to be happy. It's only necessary to be rich.

Alan Alda

It makes it fun. When an actor plays a character, you want what that character wants. Otherwise it doesn't look authentic. So I really want to defeat Jimmy - I mean Jimmy as the character.

Alan Alda

It's a funny feeling to work with people who you consider your colleagues and to realize that they actually are young enough to be your children.

Alan Alda

It's not an epitaph. I felt I could look back at my life and get a good story out of it. It's a picture of somebody trying to figure things out. I'm not trying to create some impression about myself. That doesn't interest me.

Alan Alda

It's really clear to me that you can't hang onto something longer than its time. Ideas lose certain freshness, ideas have a shelf life, and sometimes they have to be replaced by other ideas.

Alan Alda

It's too bad I'm not as wonderful a person as people say I am, because the world could use a few people like that.

Alan Alda

It's very important for us to see that science is done by people, not just brains but whole human beings, and sometimes at great cost.

Alan Alda

Kids are natural scientists.

Alan Alda

Laugh at yourself, but don't ever aim your doubt at yourself. Be bold. When you embark for strange places, don't leave any of yourself safely on shore. Have the nerve to go into unexplored territory.

Alan Alda

Listening is being able to be changed by the other person.

Alan Alda

M*A*S*H' was a collection of people, in front of and behind the cameras, that really clicked.

Alan Alda

Marie Curie is my hero. Few people have accomplished something so rare - changing science. And as hard as that is, she had to do it against the tide of the culture at the time - the prejudice against her as a foreigner, because she was born in Poland and worked in France. And the prejudice against her as a woman.

Alan Alda

Musicals are hard for me because I got thrown out of the glee club in high school, because I couldn't sing in tune at the time. I can sing in tune now, but I have to work really hard on it to make sure that I don't exercise one of my great talents, which is the ability to sing in three keys at the same time.

Alan Alda

My background is on the stage, so when I'd write movies, they'd be a lot like plays.

Alan Alda

My father sang well, and he was a handsome man. When he walked down the street, people sometimes mistook him for Cary Grant and asked for his autograph.

Alan Alda

My mother didn't try to stab my father until I was six, but she must have shown signs of oddness before that.

Alan Alda

No man or woman of the humblest sort can really be strong, gentle and good, without the world being better for it, without somebody being helped and comforted by the very existence of that goodness.

Alan Alda

No, I never thought about my image. It interests me that there are people who do, that they seem to be methodical about it.

Alan Alda

On the stage, the characters express themselves more through words than images. So the arguments of the characters and the tension between characters - words have to be used to express that, and I love that about theater.

Alan Alda

Really top-notch directors, I've often worked with them just to see how they work.

Alan Alda

Some of the greatest things, as I understand, they have come about by serendipity, the greatest discoveries.

Alan Alda

The President never intends to get into any kind of war situation. He gets carried away by events.

Alan Alda

The hardest thing for me about making movies, and that included 'M*A*S*H' because it was made like a movie, was starting and stopping.

Alan Alda

The idea that the brain is not fully formed until you are almost 30 years old has already been introduced, and the Supreme Court already has based two rulings on it.

Alan Alda

The meaning of life is life.

Alan Alda

The one thing I think I've noticed about shows that are supposed to be funny on television is that they've sort of become routinized, so there's an awful lot of mannerisms and joke lines that are sort of there to trigger laughter, rather than give actors a chance to play a moment.

Alan Alda

The thing is when you're... well-enough known, you get asked to speak places, and they don't really think about whether or not you're qualified. They just want somebody that will be a drawing card for the audience. So it's up to you to decide whether or not it's foolish to get up and speak to these people.

Alan Alda

The whole question of fiduciary responsibility is a very old concept. You could make a movie about someone making that rule at any point in history, and within a few months, it will turn out to be timely.

Alan Alda

There is a wonderful feeling of power when you're a director, but I don't think I need that, and I'm OK without it.

Alan Alda

To do a musical takes a tremendous amount of energy because you have to act and sing at the same time. And everything has to be precise. Because you can't forget the lyrics because the band keeps playing, you know, and you're under a certain amount of pressure.

Alan Alda

Usually, comedy shows only influence other comedy shows. 'M*A*S*H' is one of the few comedies that influenced dramatic shows as well.

Alan Alda

We need to be more conversant with it because science is in our lives. It's in everything. It's in the food we eat. It's in the air we breathe. It's everywhere.

Alan Alda

We're highly social animals - I'm told by scientists that what makes us different from other animals is an acute social awareness, which is what has made us so successful.

Alan Alda

What I always wanted to get seen as was as a good actor, when it was the acting I was doing. When I'm writing, I want to try to be seen as a good writer. Not as somebody with a particular idea to sell, or something like that.

Alan Alda

What I always wanted to get seen as was as a good actor, when it was the acting I was doing. When I'm writing, I want to try to be seen as a good writer.

Alan Alda

What I can't completely understand is most other people's fascination with what the famous among us do with their lips and the rest of their bodies. Why do ordinary people become the target of this curiosity simply by virtue of the fact that other people recognise their names and faces but know almost nothing else about them?

Alan Alda

What heartens me is to see '30 Rock' on the air. It makes me laugh from my gut, which I really like to do.

Alan Alda

What is beauty, anyway? It's more than something pleasant looking. If it doesn't stop us in our tracks and make us unable to move for a moment, unable to put into words what's closing off the breath in our throats, then maybe it's pretty, but it probably isn't beauty.

Alan Alda

When I am at a dinner table, I love to ask everybody, 'How long do you think our species might last?' I've read that the average age of a species, of any species, is about two million years. Is it possible we can have an average life span as a species? And do you picture us two million years more or a million and a half years, or 5,000?

Alan Alda

When I got recognized as a writer, when I got the Emmy, I was more excited than the Emmys I had gotten as an actor.

Alan Alda

When I was about ten years old, I gave my teacher an April Fool's sandwich, which had a dead goldfish in it.

Alan Alda

When I was in high school, I fell under the spell of that crazy idea that if you're interested in the arts, you can't be interested in science.

Alan Alda

When does she do all this thinking? We're together all the time but she thinks deeply about things and with feeling and she can remember the facts. We've been married 48 years.

Alan Alda

When people are laughing, they're generally not killing one another.

Alan Alda

Whenever I think of how much pleasure I have interviewing scientists, I remember that they're having the real fun in actually being able to do the science.

Alan Alda

Why would you give money to somebody whose work you don't understand?

Alan Alda

You can watch actors create their illusions, but if you don't see where they get the pigeons from, you don't really know how they're doing it.

Alan Alda

You can't be aware of everything. You'd fall down the stairs if you were aware of every intricate thing involved in going down stairs.

Alan Alda

You can't get there by bus, only by hard work and risk and by not quite knowing what you're doing. What you'll discover will be wonderful. What you'll discover will be yourself.

Alan Alda

You have to leave the city of your comfort and go into the wilderness of your intuition. What you'll discover will be wonderful. What you'll discover is yourself.

Alan Alda

You know what my earliest memories are? Going from one burlesque town to another. My father was in burlesque.

Alan Alda

You wouldn't want to be called a sell-out by selling a product. Selling out was frowned on, whereas now you can major in it at business school.

Alan Alda

This page is intentionally left blank

This page is intentionally left blank

This page is intentionally left blank

This page is intentionally left blank

This page is intentionally left blank

www.ingramcontent.com/pod-product-compliance
Lightning Source LLC
Chambersburg PA
CBHW061932280526
45787CB00004B/1581